THE

Word

...given them out of their distresses.

20 He sent his word, and healed them, and delivered them from their destructions.

21 Oh that men would praise the Lord for his...

CATHY DUPLANTIS

The Healing Word
ISBN 0-9743829-7-3
Copyright ©2005 Cathy Duplantis
Published by Jesse Duplantis Ministries
4th Printing 2014

Jesse Duplantis Ministries
PO Box 1089
Destrehan, Louisiana 70047
USA
www.jdm.org

Jesse Duplantis Ministries is dedicated to reaching people and changing lives with the Gospel of Jesus Christ. For more information, or to purchase other products from Jesse Duplantis Ministries, please contact us at the address above.

*"He sent His Word, and healed them,
and delivered them from their destructions."*
(Psalm 107:20)

*This book is lovingly dedicated
to my mother, Irene*

What Do You Really Want?

In the days that Jesus walked the earth, crowds of desperate people sought Him out because they had heard the word about His power to heal the sick and deliver the oppressed. Luke 6:19 tells us, *"And the whole multitude sought to touch Him: for there went virtue out of Him, and **healed them all**."* Throughout all of the land, families carried their loved ones on stretchers to get what they wanted from Jesus and they were not disappointed.

Did you ever notice how often Jesus asked people what they wanted Him to do for them? The leper, the lame man by the pool, the woman with the demon possessed daughter, and the woman with the issue of blood all spoke with Jesus about what they wanted from Him. Their voice was connected to a door of their heart that was filled with faith in God's Word. Regardless of the opposition they faced on the road to their healing, they refused to give up and kept pressing in for the promise.

The best example of this method of Jesus' ministry was in the healing of blind Bartimaeus sitting by the roadside near Jericho. Now, this was not the only time that Jesus was interrupted by a desperate person in the road. Therefore, it is clear from God's Word that faith always gets the attention of God.

Bartimaeus apparently had heard that the Messiah had come, and he was determined to get what he wanted from God. He could care less if the crowd that surrounded Jesus that day did not want to hear his cry for help. He refused to give up and began to shout even louder! He pressed on in faith and got the attention of Jesus.

Have you ever wondered what would have happened to that old blind man if he had given up when opposition came against him? People can be very cruel. He may have been ridiculed for believing that he, of all people, would get noticed by the Master and be healed.

What Are You Saying?

Many people have been offended and given up with much less persecution than Bartimaeus endured that day. But, when it comes to healing, God is not interested in what others are saying; He wants to know what *you* are saying about *your* healing.

He has given you His Word that can not fail, that will not return void, and will never pass away. Be determined to search out the healing promises in God's Word and put yourself in the verses like those found in Exodus 15:26, Deuteronomy 7:15, Isaiah 53:4-5, 1 Peter 2:24, Psalm 103:3, and begin to boldly declare: "My God is the Lord who heals me! He will take all sickness away from me! Surely He has born my sickness and pain and by His stripes I am healed! My God heals all my diseases!" Be determined to press forward in faith, and you *will* get whatsoever you desire from God!

When Bartimaeus heard that the Master had called him, he immediately threw off his cloak, or outer garment, which signified that he was blind and destined to beg for the rest of his life. Then, he leaped up and came to Jesus fully expecting to receive what he wanted. By his actions, Bartimaeus was declaring that he would never need that old cloak again. Once he was healed, he would be able to work and would never be broke another day in his life. By throwing off that old cloak, he demonstrated his refusal to tolerate anything that would hinder him from getting to Jesus.

God Is Moved By Faith!

Now, everyone must have guessed what that old beggar wanted when the Miracle Worker walked through the village that day. Yet, Mark 10:51 tells us, *"And Jesus said to him, **What do you want** Me to do for you? And the blind man said to Him, Master, let me receive my sight"* (Amplified). You see, God is not moved by need, He is moved by faith. Even though Jesus knew what Bartimaeus needed, he was waiting for a specific request and an expression of true faith.

It is clear that the main principle of prayer is ask, seek, and knock. In Matthew 7:7-8 Jesus told us, *"Ask, and it shall be given you; seek, and ye shall find; knock, and it shall be opened unto you: For every one that asketh receiveth; and he that seeketh findeth; and to him that knocketh it shall be opened."*

Faith in God's Word will always be rewarded, regardless of what the need is or how impossible it seems. That is what Bartimaeus discovered one day on that dusty Jericho road.

Jesus told him, *"Go thy way; **thy faith hath made thee whole**. And immediately he **received his sight**, and followed Jesus in the way"* (Mark 10:52).

Faith in God and His Word will ask, seek, and knock until everything is received, found, and opened. Refuse to give up on your healing. Meditate on the four steps in *The Healing Word* so that it will flood your heart and mind with faith to make you whole.

Be determined to get what you want. Begin to push away obstacles that are designed by the devil to keep you down. Refuse to settle for less than God's best. No matter what you need in life, you can learn how to depend on a God that *"...is able to do exceeding abundantly above all that we ask or think, according to the power that worketh in us"* (Ephesians 3:20).

Matthew 4:23 *And Jesus went about all Galilee, teaching in their synagogues, and preaching the Gospel of the kingdom, and **healing all manner of sickness and all manner of disease among the people**.*

Matthew 8:16-17 When the even was come, they brought unto Him many that were possessed with devils: and He cast out the spirits with His word, and **healed all** that were sick:

That it might be fulfilled which was spoken by Esaias the prophet, saying, Himself took **our** infirmities, and bare **our** sicknesses.

Matthew 9:35 *And Jesus went about all the cities and villages, teaching in their synagogues, and preaching the Gospel of the kingdom, and **healing every sickness and every disease among the people.***

Mark 1:40-42 *And there came a leper to Him, beseeching Him, and kneeling down to Him, and saying unto Him, **If thou wilt, thou canst make me clean.***

*And Jesus, moved with compassion, put forth His hand, and touched Him, and saith unto Him, **I will**; be thou clean.*

And as soon as He had spoken, immediately the leprosy departed from him, and he was cleansed.

John 6:38 *For I came down from heaven, not to do Mine own will, but the will of Him that sent Me.*

Hebrews 13:8 *Jesus Christ the same yesterday, and to day, and for ever.*

3 John 2 *Beloved, I wish above all things that thou mayest prosper **and be in health**, even as thy soul prospereth.*

Mark 6:56 And whithersoever He entered, into villages, or cities, or country, they laid the sick in the streets, and besought Him that they might touch if it were but the border of His garment: and **as many as touched Him** were made whole.

Acts 10:34-38 *Then Peter opened his mouth, and said, Of a truth I perceive that God is no respecter of persons:*

But in every nation he that feareth Him, and worketh righteousness, is accepted with Him.

The Word which God sent unto the children of Israel, preaching peace by Jesus Christ: (He is Lord of all:)

That Word, I say, ye know, which was published throughout all Judaea, and began from Galilee, after the baptism which John preached;

*How God anointed Jesus of Nazareth with the Holy Ghost and with power: who went about doing good, **and healing all that were oppressed of the devil;** for God was with Him.*

Isaiah 53:4-5 *Surely He hath borne our griefs, and carried our sorrows: yet we did esteem Him stricken, smitten of God, and afflicted.*

But He was wounded for our transgressions, He was bruised for our iniquities: the chastisement of our peace was upon Him; and with His stripes we are healed.

1 Peter 2:24 *Who His own self bare our sins in His own body on the tree, that we, being dead to sins, should live unto righteousness: by Whose stripes ye were healed.*

*Realize That Healing
is Received by Faith
Based on God's Word*

Romans 10:17 *So then faith cometh by hearing, and hearing by the Word of God.*

Hebrews 11:1 *Now faith is the assurance (the confirmation, the title deed) of the things [we] hope for, being the proof of things [we] do not see and the conviction of their reality [faith perceiving as real fact what is not revealed to the senses] (AMP).*

Mark 11:22-24** And Jesus answering saith unto them, **Have faith in God.

*For verily I say unto you, That **whosoever shall say** unto this mountain, Be thou removed, and be thou cast into the sea; and shall not doubt in his heart, but shall believe that those things which **he saith** shall come to pass; he shall have **whatsoever he saith**.*

*Therefore I say unto you, What things soever **ye desire**, when ye pray, believe that ye receive them, and ye shall have them.*

Psalm 37:4 Delight *thyself also in the LORD; and He shall give thee the* **desires of thine heart**.

John 15:7 *If ye abide in Me, and* **My Words abide in you***, ye shall* **ask what ye will***, and it shall be done unto you.*

Matthew 7:7-11 *Ask, and it shall be given you; seek, and ye shall find; knock, and it shall be opened unto you:*

For every one that asketh receiveth; and he that seeketh findeth; and to him that knocketh it shall be opened.

Or what man is there of you, whom if his son ask bread, will he give him a stone?

Or if he ask a fish, will he give him a serpent?

If ye then, being evil, know how to give good gifts unto your children, how much more shall your Father which is in heaven give good things to them that ask Him?

Mark 5:25-34 And a certain woman, which had an issue of blood twelve years,

And had suffered many things of many physicians, and had spent all that she had, and was nothing bettered, but rather grew worse,

When she had **heard** of Jesus, **came** in the press behind, and **touched** His garment.

For she said, If I may touch but His clothes, I shall be whole.

And straightway the fountain of her blood was dried up; and she felt in her body that she was healed of that plague.

And Jesus, immediately knowing in Himself that virtue had gone out of Him, turned Him about in the press, and said, Who touched My clothes?

And His disciples said unto Him, Thou seest the multitude thronging Thee, and sayest Thou, Who touched Me?

And He looked round about to see her that had done this thing.

But the woman fearing and trembling, knowing what was done in her, came and fell down before Him, and told Him all the truth.

And He said unto her, Daughter, **thy faith hath made thee whole**; go in peace, and be whole of thy plague.

Luke 5:17-26 And it came to pass on a certain day, as He was teaching, that there were Pharisees and doctors of the law sitting by, which were come out of every town of Galilee, and Judaea, and Jerusalem: **and the power of the Lord was present to heal them.**

And, behold, men brought in a bed a man which was taken with a palsy: and they sought means to bring him in, and to lay him before Him.

And when they could not find by what way they might bring him in because of the multitude, they went upon the housetop, and let him down through the tiling with his couch into the midst before Jesus.

And when He saw their faith, He said unto him, Man, thy sins are forgiven thee.

And the scribes and the Pharisees began to reason, saying, Who is this which speaketh blasphemies? Who can forgive sins, but God alone?

But when Jesus perceived their thoughts, He answering said unto them, What reason ye in your hearts?

Whether is easier, to say, Thy sins be forgiven thee; or to say, Rise up and walk?

*But that ye may know that the Son of man hath power upon earth to forgive sins, (He said unto the sick of the palsy,) I say unto thee, **Arise, and take up thy couch, and go into thine house.***

And immediately he rose up before them, and took up that whereon he lay, and departed to his own house, glorifying God.

And they were all amazed, and they glorified God, and were filled with fear, saying, We have seen strange things to day.

Luke 6:17-19 *And He came down with them, and stood in the plain, and the company of His disciples, and a great multitude of people out of all Judaea and Jerusalem, and from the sea coast of Tyre and Sidon, which came to hear Him, and to be healed of their diseases;*

And they that were vexed with unclean spirits: and they were healed.

And the whole multitude sought to touch Him: for there went virtue out of Him, and healed them all.

Luke 7:1-10 *Now when He had ended all His sayings in the audience of the people, He entered into Capernaum.*

And a certain centurion's servant, who was dear unto him, was sick, and ready to die.

And when he heard of Jesus, he sent unto him the elders of the Jews, beseeching Him that He would come and heal his servant.

And when they came to Jesus, they besought Him instantly, saying, That he was worthy for whom He should do this:

For he loveth our nation, and he hath built us a synagogue.

Then Jesus went with them. And when He was now not far from the house, the centurion sent friends to Him, saying unto Him, Lord, trouble not Thyself: for I am not worthy that Thou shouldest enter under my roof:

Wherefore neither thought I myself worthy to come unto Thee: **but say in a word, and my servant shall be healed.**

For I also am a man set under authority, having under me soldiers, and I say unto one, Go, and he goeth; and to another, Come, and he cometh; and to my servant, Do this, and he doeth it.

When Jesus heard these things, He marvelled at him, and turned him about, and said unto the people that followed Him, I say unto you, **I have not found so great faith**, *no, not in Israel.*

And they that were sent, returning to the house, found the servant whole that had been sick.

Luke 13:11-17 *And, behold, there was a woman which had a spirit of infirmity eighteen years, and was bowed together, and could in no wise lift up herself.*

And when Jesus saw her, He called her to Him, and said unto her, Woman, thou art loosed from thine infirmity.

And He laid His hands on her: and immediately she was made straight, and glorified God.

And the ruler of the synagogue answered with indignation, because that Jesus had healed on the sabbath day, and said unto the people, There are six days in which men ought to work: in them therefore come and be healed, and not on the sabbath day.

The Lord then answered him, and said, Thou hypocrite, doth not each one of you on the sabbath loose his ox or his ass from the stall, and lead him away to watering?

And ought not this woman, being a daughter of Abraham, whom Satan hath bound, lo, these eighteen years, be loosed from this bond on the sabbath day?

And when He had said these things, all His adversaries were ashamed: and all the people rejoiced for all the glorious things that were done by Him.

Acts 3:1-8 *Now Peter and John went up together into the temple at the hour of prayer, being the ninth hour.*

And a certain man lame from his mother's womb was carried, whom they laid daily at the gate of the temple which is called Beautiful, to ask alms of them that entered into the temple;

Who seeing Peter and John about to go into the temple asked an alms.

And Peter, fastening his eyes upon him with John, said, Look on us.

And he gave heed unto them, expecting to receive something of them.

Then Peter said, Silver and gold have I none; but such as I have give I thee: In the name of Jesus Christ of Nazareth rise up and walk.

And he took him by the right hand, and lifted him up: and immediately his feet and ankle bones received strength.

And he leaping up stood, and walked, and entered with them into the temple, walking, and leaping, and praising God.

Acts 9:32-35 *And it came to pass, as Peter passed throughout all quarters, he came down also to the saints which dwelt at Lydda.*

And there he found a certain man named Aeneas, which had kept his bed eight years, and was sick of the palsy.

And Peter said unto him, Aeneas, Jesus Christ maketh thee whole: arise, and make thy bed. And he arose immediately.

And all that dwelt at Lydda and Saron saw him, and turned to the Lord.

Acts

Acts 9:36-42 *Now there was at Joppa a certain disciple named Tabitha, which by interpretation is called Dorcas: this woman was full of good works and almsdeeds which she did.*

And it came to pass in those days, that she was sick, and died: whom when they had washed, they laid her in an upper chamber.

And forasmuch as Lydda was nigh to Joppa, and the disciples had heard that Peter was there, they sent unto him two men, desiring him that he would not delay to come to them.

Then Peter arose and went with them. When he was come, they brought him into the upper chamber: and all the widows stood by him weeping, and shewing the coats and garments which Dorcas made, while she was with them.

But Peter put them all forth, and kneeled down, and prayed; and turning him to the body said, Tabitha, arise. And she opened her eyes: and when she saw Peter, she sat up.

And he gave her his hand, and lifted her up, and when he had called the saints and widows, presented her alive.

And it was known throughout all Joppa; and many believed in the Lord.

Acts 14:8-10 *And there sat a certain man at Lystra, impotent in his feet, being a cripple from his mother's womb, who never had walked:*

The same heard Paul speak: who stedfastly beholding him, and perceiving that **he had faith to be healed,**

Said with a loud voice, Stand upright on thy feet. And he leaped and walked.

John 6:63 *It is the spirit that quickeneth; the flesh profiteth nothing: **the words that I speak unto you, they are spirit, and they are life.***

Step Three

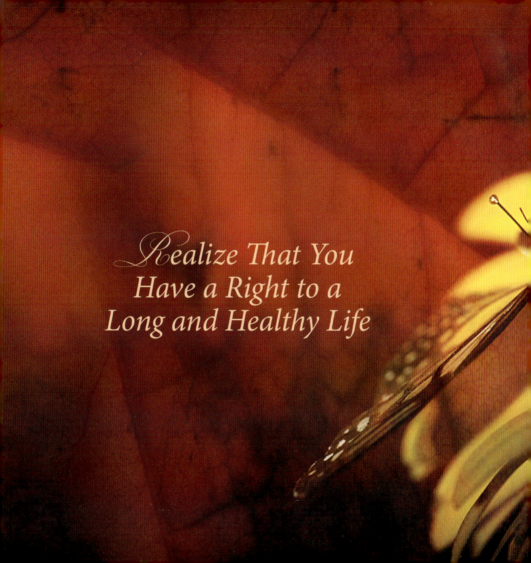

Realize That You Have a Right to a Long and Healthy Life

Genesis 6:3 *And the LORD said, My spirit shall not always strive with man, for that he also is flesh:* **yet his days shall be an hundred and twenty years.**

Exodus 15:26 *And said, If thou wilt diligently hearken to the voice of the LORD thy God, and wilt do that which is right in His sight, and wilt give ear to His commandments, and keep all His statutes, I will put none of these diseases upon thee, which I have brought upon the Egyptians: for I am the LORD that healeth thee.*

Exodus 23:25-26 *And ye shall serve the LORD your God, and He shall bless thy bread, and thy water; and I will take sickness away from the midst of thee...the number of thy days I will fulfil.*

Deuteronomy 7:15 *And the LORD will take away from thee all sickness....*

Deuteronomy 30:19-20 *I call heaven and earth to record this day against you, that I have set before you life and death, blessing and cursing: therefore choose life, that both thou and thy seed may live: That thou mayest love the LORD thy God, and that thou mayest obey His voice, and that thou mayest cleave unto Him: for He is thy life, and the length of thy days: that thou mayest dwell in the land which the LORD sware unto thy fathers, to Abraham, to Isaac, and to Jacob, to give them.*

Deuteronomy 32:47 *For it is not a vain thing for you; because it is your life: and through this thing ye shall prolong your days in the land, whither ye go over Jordan to possess it.*

Deuteronomy 34:7 *And Moses was an hundred and twenty years old when he died: his eye was not dim, nor his natural force abated.*

Psalm 91:16 *With long life will I satisfy him, and shew him My salvation.*

Proverbs 3:1-2 *My son, forget not My law; but let thine heart keep My commandments:*
For length of days, and long life, and peace, shall they add to thee.

Proverbs 4:20-23 *My son, **attend to My words**; incline thine ear unto My sayings.*

Let them not depart from thine eyes; keep them in the midst of thine heart.

*For they are **life** unto those that find them, and **health** to all their flesh.*

Keep thy heart with all diligence; for out of it are the issues of life.

Romans 8:2 *For the law of the Spirit of life in Christ Jesus hath made me free from the law of sin and death.*

Romans 8:11 But if the Spirit of Him that raised up Jesus from the dead dwell in you, He that raised up Christ from the dead shall also quicken your mortal bodies by His Spirit that dwelleth in you.

Step Four

*Express Your Thankfulness
to God for
His Healing Word*

Luke 17:11-19 *And it came to pass, as He went to Jerusalem, that He passed through the midst of Samaria and Galilee.*

And as He entered into a certain village, there met Him ten men that were lepers, which stood afar off:

And they lifted up their voices, and said, Jesus, Master, have mercy on us.

And when He saw them, He said unto them, Go shew yourselves unto the priests. And it came to pass, that, as they went, they were cleansed.

And one of them, when he saw that he was healed, turned back, and with a loud voice glorified God,

And fell down on his face at His feet, **giving Him thanks**: and he was a Samaritan.

And Jesus answering said, Were there not ten cleansed? but where are the nine?

There are not found that returned to give glory to God, save this stranger.

And He said unto him, Arise, go thy way: **thy faith** hath made thee whole.

Philippians 4:6-7 *Be careful for nothing; but in every thing by prayer and supplication with thanksgiving let your requests be made known unto God.*

And the peace of God, which passeth all understanding, shall keep your hearts and minds through Christ Jesus.

Colossians 3:15 *And let the peace of God rule in your hearts, to the which also ye are called in one body; and be ye thankful.*

Psalm 100:1-5 *Make a joyful noise unto the LORD, all ye lands.*

Serve the LORD with gladness: come before His presence with singing.

Know ye that the LORD He is God: it is He that hath made us, and not we ourselves; we are His people, and the sheep of His pasture.

Enter into His gates with thanksgiving, and into His courts with praise: be thankful unto Him, and bless His name.

For the LORD is good; His mercy is everlasting; and His truth endureth to all generations.

Psalm 103:1-5 *Bless the LORD, O my soul: and all that is within me, bless His holy name.*

Bless the LORD, O my soul, and forget not all His benefits:

Who forgiveth all thine iniquities; **Who healeth all thy diseases;**

Who redeemeth thy life from destruction; *Who crowneth thee with lovingkindness and tender mercies;*

Who satisfieth thy mouth with good things; so that **thy youth is renewed** *like the eagle's.*

Choose Life and Live

The third chapter of the Gospel of John records the encounter of a Pharisee named Nicodemus with Jesus one night. In verse two, he said to Jesus, *"...Rabbi, **we know** that thou art a teacher come from God: for no man can do these miracles that thou doest, except God be with him."* Jesus' reply in verse three to this very religious man was, *"...Verily, verily, I say unto thee, Except a man be born again, he cannot **see** the kingdom of God"* (John 3:3).

At first glance at that passage, I wondered why Jesus responded that way. Nicodemus didn't seem to ask that question. But after closer study, I discovered that the word *"see"* in verse three is the same Greek word, "eido" which means "to know" that was translated *"know"* in verse two. That Pharisee claimed *"to know"* what was going on, but Jesus gave Nick a quick reality check that night. Verse three in the Amplified Bible really makes this clear, *"...I assure you, most solemnly I tell you, that unless a person is born again (anew, from above), he cannot ever see (**know**, be acquainted with, and experience) the kingdom of God."*

Nicodemus had attended the finest schools of his day and was a ruler of the Jews, yet he could not comprehend this basic kingdom truth. He was faced with the same choice as every one else, *"...Ye must be born again"* (John 3:7). It was the only way that he could **know** how God's kingdom operates. 1 Corinthians 2:14 says, *"But the natural man receiveth not the things of the Spirit of God: for they are foolishness* *unto him: neither can he know them, because they are spiritually discerned."*

The reverse of that statement is also true. Cathy's translation: "The spiritual man **receiveth** the things of the Spirit of God: for they are **wisdom** unto him, and he can **know** them because he can spiritually discern the things of God." If you have accepted Jesus as your Savior, you have been spiritually born again and can receive the things of God. You can know the things that have been freely given to you by God (1 Corinthians 2:12). You can expect God's Word to instruct you in all wisdom and guide your steps (Colossians 1:9; John 16:4; Proverbs 3:6; Psalm 37:23).

When you choose God and His Word, you are actually choosing life. Jesus said, *"... the **Words** that I speak unto you, they are spirit, and **they are life"** (John 6:63). There is really no way to separate the Word of God from the life of God. His Words are life! Proverbs 4:20-22 says, *"My son, attend to My words; incline thine ear unto My sayings. Let them not depart from thine eyes; keep them in the midst of thine heart. For they are life unto those that find them, and health to all their flesh."*

Perhaps you are looking for a new start in life. It is never too late to choose life and live. If you are ready to acknowledge the choices that have led you down your dead-end street, you can change. It really is up to you.

Your salvation is as simple as ABC:

Admit you are a sinner.
Believe that Jesus died for your sins.
Confess that Jesus is your Savior.

Romans 10:9-13 says, *"That if thou shalt **confess with thy mouth the Lord Jesus**, and shalt **believe in thine heart** that God hath raised Him from the dead, **thou shalt be saved**. For with the heart man believeth unto righteousness; and with the mouth confession is made unto salvation. For the scripture saith, Whosoever believeth on Him shall not be ashamed. For there is no difference between the Jew and the Greek: for the same Lord over all is rich unto all that call upon Him. For whosoever shall call upon the name of the Lord shall be saved."*

Wise living involves learning to assess the value of choices and choosing those things that have lasting impact or value. Jesus and His Word are the only ways to transform a dead, meaningless existence into a life filled with joy, peace, and purpose. It is the only choice that will last for eternity.

Choose **Jesus** today.
Choose **health**.
Choose **life** and live!

Other Books in This Series
by Cathy Duplantis
The Peaceful Word (Book and CD)

Other Books

How to Behave in a Cave

Keeping a Clean Heart

To contact Cathy Duplantis
write or call:

Jesse Duplantis Ministries
PO Box 1089
Destrehan, Louisiana 70047
(985) 764-2000

Or visit us online at:
www.jdm.org

*Please include your prayer requests
and praise reports when you write.*